Copyright © 2021 Mark Greenwood

revmarkgreenwood.com

Twitter @revgreenie

Published for Mark Greenwood in 2021
by Verité CM Limited
www.veritecm.com

The right of Mark Greenwood to be identified as the author of this work has been asserted by him in accordance with the Copyright, Designs and Patents Act 1988.

ISBN: 978-1-914388-10-1

All rights reserved. No part of this publication may be reproduced or transmitted in any form or by any means, electronic or mechanical including photocopying, recording, or any information storage and retrieval system, without prior permission in writing from the author.

Printed in England

Designed by Ashdown Creative
Proofread by Louise Stenhouse

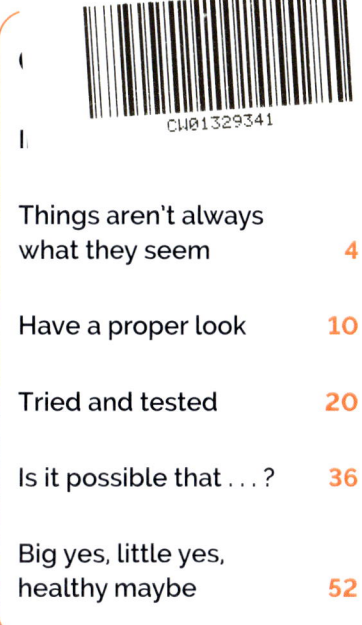

Things aren't always what they seem	4
Have a proper look	10
Tried and tested	20
Is it possible that . . . ?	36
Big yes, little yes, healthy maybe	52

It has been estimated that knowledge is exploding at such a rate – more than 2,000 pages a minute – that even Einstein couldn't keep up. In fact, if you read 24 hours a day from age 21 to 70 and retained all you read, you would be one and a half million years behind by the time you finished.

(*Campus Life*, February, 1979)

Dear reader,

I love learning more about the things I already know about, and the older I get I love to learn a whole bunch of new things I don't know too. The thing is, the more I learn, the more I realise how much there is still to learn and it's with this attitude I try to face life and faith.

I try to be open minded precisely because I don't know everything. In fact I often think I know very little! I believe that if I am going to learn about things, I need to get beneath the surface that I might begin to truly understand something, or even someone. I need to look differently at things as well as deeper into things. To be willing to go beyond what I already think about things and sometimes to take a step back and see the bigger picture. It's sort of a quantity of knowledge and quality of knowledge – a breadth and depth if you will.

The aim of *Is it Possible?* is to invite you on a journey to learn, and to gently challenge you to become open minded about God and Christianity and, in doing so, discover what you don't know as well as what you do know.

I'll share with you some things that have made me smile, some things that intrigue me, some things I have discovered.

Would you be willing to come with me?

Yours in the search,

MARK GREENWOOD

Things aren't always what they seem

> **A museum in County Durham had to stop displaying a Roman coin from the second century AD as a 9-year-old boy correctly identified it as a plastic token given away in a soft-drinks promotion.**
>
> **Jubilant experts thought they'd found a 1,000-year-old Viking settlement buried in a back garden. For days they carefully peeled earth from the ancient slabs. Then the truth dawned – it was a sunken patio built in the 1940s.**
>
> **Armed police dashed to a West Midlands bank after a passer-by spotted staff sheltering under desks . . . only to discover it was a "team-building" game of hide-and-seek. A member of the public called 999 after spotting people in the window of NatWest. Armed police attended the branch in Birmingham but did not find a burglary.**

Have you ever got the wrong end of the stick about someone or something? Have you ever had to change your mind about someone or something? Have you ever been frustrated by how someone has made a judgement about you without really getting to know you?

Is it possible that you may have the wrong end of the stick when it comes to Christianity, God and Jesus? That you have made a judgement about it all, without having any real experience of him?

It may be that you have had negative experiences about the church but let me encourage you that things aren't always what they seem.

Is it Possible?

The lighthouse and US Navy ship

This is the transcript of a radio conversation between a US Navy ship and Canadian authorities off the coast of Newfoundland in October 1995.

Americans:	Please divert your course 15 degrees to the north to avoid a collision.
Canadians:	Recommend you divert YOUR course 15 degrees to the south to avoid a collision.
Americans:	This is the captain of a US Navy ship. I say again, divert YOUR course.
Canadians:	No. I say again, you divert YOUR course.
Americans:	This is the aircraft carrier USS *Lincoln*, the second largest ship in the United States' Atlantic fleet. We are accompanied by three destroyers, three cruisers and numerous support vessels. I demand that YOU change your course 15 degrees north, that's one-five degrees north, or countermeasures will be undertaken to ensure the safety of this ship.
Canadians:	This is a lighthouse. Your call.

Radio conversation released by the Chief of Naval Operations, 10th October 1995.

Is it Possible?

Always one for a giggle and seeing the more fun side of life, I never looked at Christianity and ever saw it as something other than miserable. My first three experiences of church were not good: a christening, a wedding and a funeral did not help change my perceptions of church and therefore God. My christening I don't remember, the wedding was boring and the funeral was depressing. Would you blame me if I never went to church again?

It was only when I went along the fourth time that I realised "things aren't always what they seem". I met people from all walks of life, who genuinely followed Jesus. I saw up close and personal – I looked from a different perspective and I am so glad I did. They had what I wanted.

Sometimes you have to be prepared to change your mind.

Is it Possible?

I'm fond of a banoffee

Many years ago I was out walking with a friend in the beautiful Cotswolds. We came across a lovely tearoom and I could see it there in the window, smiling at me, calling me in: the biggest banoffee pie I had ever seen. Now you need to understand I absolutely love banoffee pie, I mean really love it. I announced with the enthusiasm of a 5-year-old child, "Come on, we are having banoffee pie!" I mean, I was going to buy my friend some, too. My heart sank when he told me he didn't like it. Not only that but the reason he gave. The conversation went something like this:

Me:	Yessssssss, banoffee pie! Let me buy you some banoffee pie.
Him:	Erm, I don't like banoffee pie.
Me:	Why don't you like banoffee pie?
Him:	Because I don't like coffee.
Me:	But you don't have to have coffee with it, you can have a cup of tea or a cold drink.
Him:	No, the coffee is in the banoffee!
Me:	You think that banoffee has coffee in it?

Is it Possible?

Him:	Yes, the offee.
Me:	No, the offee in banoffee is not the offee that's in coffee; the offee in banoffee is the offee that's in toffee.

I couldn't believe it; he'd not tried a single piece of banoffee pie because of what he thought was in it. But it wasn't.

It is easy to be put off something because of what we think it is, or what it consists of. Is it possible that you may have got God, Jesus and Christianity wrong? That you may be missing out on something that is amazing because of a perception.

My mum once said to me, "You don't miss what you've never had." Well, of course that's true but I would say, "Why miss out when you can have it?"

Never say never when you've never tried it. You may just be missing out on the treat of your life!

You will read this first

And then you will read this

Then this one

Is it Possible?

See the full picture

It's easy to get fixated on one aspect or difficulty of the Christian faith, and because you can't get your head around it, you end up not seeing the full picture.

Is it Possible?

It's only when you see the full picture that you begin to get a true perspective.

Can you guess what these images are? See the full pictures in all their detail on page 56.

Jona Jacob www.jjacobphotography.co.uk

Is it Possible?

Try to see from a different perspective

I remember trying to help someone see a tower on the horizon that I could see but they couldn't. When no amount of explaining helped I stood behind them and moved their head to the right point. "Ahhhhh! I can see it now!" they exclaimed.

Sometimes you have to look from a different angle and that may involve people helping you to do so over time.

Is it Possible?

16

I just couldn't see what she saw

I remember first coming across "magic eye" images. At first I couldn't see the images that others could see. I remember on one occasion, the person trying to convince me to look was so enthusiastic and so I looked (even though I had tried many times before and was a tad cynical).

They kept on telling me to "look properly", "let your eyes fall into the image".

I became frustrated as I just couldn't see it. They went but left the image propped up by the side of a chair. I couldn't resist – this time it was my decision. I picked it up and looked, and I couldn't believe it: I could see it! It's like it just seemed to appear.

I immediately ran with it to find someone else in the building. I made them look, much to their protestations. I was so disappointed as they just couldn't see it! Despite my telling them to "look closely", "look properly", "let your eyes fall into the image".

You see, I couldn't see it but then, through taking time to look properly, I could, and now I wanted everyone to see it.

Is it Possible?

Most people reject Christianity without actually knowing much about it and without looking into it. If you believe that Jesus is not for you, make sure you are rejecting what he really is rather than what you think he is. Make an informed decision not an uninformed decision.

One of my friends often says,

> **"Most people's understanding of Christianity is actually a misunderstanding."**

If you agree that things aren't always what they seem, is there a possibility that you might not have quite understood what Christianity is? Is it worth a proper look?

Maybe a look from a different perspective? Maybe a look at the full picture rather than a fixation of one facet? Maybe a deeper look? Maybe a fresh look? Maybe an open-minded look?

Ways to look properly

Got questions about life?	What do you Hope for?	Want to hear some Really Good News?

alpha.org.uk	hopespaces.com	elim.org.uk/reallygoodnews

Is it Possible?

A Christian was preaching at Speakers' Corner in London, a place known for hecklers. He was in full flow when someone shouted out, "Christianity has been around for centuries and look at the mess we're are in." Noticing that the man was less than clean the preacher replied,

"Soap has been around for a lot longer than that, and look at the muck on your face."

You see, it doesn't matter how long something has been around, if it isn't applied it will have no impact whatsoever. When Christianity is applied, the impact is incredible.

One way to have a proper look into Christianity is to see the difference it has made to the lives of people who have applied it and tried it.

21

Jason tried it...

Jason Heron had no church background but after an encounter with God in a church service where he had gone to cause trouble, a journey of discovery started that would radically change his life forever.

So what was the process of my faith journey? I'm from a Romany Gypsy family. The only vague interest in God I can remember was the series *Jesus of Nazareth* on television. As I watched the programme and saw people rejecting Jesus, I thought to myself that if I was there at the time I would have believed in him, although I'm not really sure why I thought this. My only other connection was that I was given a Gideon's New Testament at school and I would say the Lord's Prayer occasionally, but that was it.

"The main reason I accepted the invitation was to cause trouble."

At home after a night out clubbing, a voice in my head told me that if I looked in the mirror I would see the devil. I felt the real presence of evil in the room. The fear that gripped my life at that moment caused me to reach for the Gideon's Bible. As I read it, the presence left me and a different presence entered. This was just a few weeks before I was invited to church.

Is it Possible?

My dad and brother-in-law had attended church and both had made a decision to become Christians. The main reason I accepted the invitation was to cause trouble. I wanted to get back at my dad as at the time our relationship was not at its best. I arrived at church with four of my friends. Apart from weddings and funerals this was the first time I'd attended church. The songs were different from what I expected and the people in the meeting looked really happy. When the singing finished we were invited to be seated.

I was just about ready to disturb the meeting and then leave so my dad would be embarrassed when a man came to the stage. When he began to talk about Jesus a weird feeling started inside me. I became very emotional and very confused; I was at the point of tears and I didn't know why.

As the speaker continued I heard him say that Jesus could give real meaning to life as well as his peace and purpose. At that moment it was as though he was speaking to me about my life. I had money, cars, great holidays, friends and a loving family, and yet I was still not fulfilled – it all left me feeling lonely and insecure.

"I experienced a weight suddenly lifting from me and I knew that he was real. From that night my life was never the same again."

At the end of his sermon the speaker asked if there was anyone who would like to give their life to Jesus. At that moment I left my seat to walk to the front of the church. I remember saying that if God was real, not to let me leave the church the same. I experienced a weight suddenly lifting from me and I knew that he was real. From that night my life was never the same again.

Rich tried it . . .

Ashamed of who he had become, Rich Old was challenged to have a proper look at the Christian faith, and when he did he realised all his preconceived ideas were far from the truth of what it actually was.

Faith played absolutely no part in the first forty years of my life. My upbringing was very non-Christian. I've made plenty of bad choices, mixed with a few "unsavoury" and even toxic people and got into some unpleasant situations along the way. I was ashamed of who I'd become and had developed a strong dislike of myself. I'd built a thick layer of armour to deal with the failings, guilt and bitterness that lay on my shoulders.

Despite the baggage I was carrying, I somehow managed to marry Marie, the one person I'd known for years who knew Jesus, but my "armour" was beginning to flake away and the "act" of being happy was becoming harder to maintain. My confidence and self-esteem had long gone and a deep depression had crept up on me and taken hold.

By the end of 2016 the unshakeable dark clouds had descended and choked any remaining hope. I was lost and unable to cope. Marie had begun to attend church. She'd suggested that I join her on several occasions but I'd been dismissive. However, I needed to be with my family, so one Sunday I decided to go to church. I didn't know what to expect, I just wanted to support Marie.

Is it Possible?

I didn't pay much attention to the sermon and if anyone talked to me afterwards I'd tell folks that Christianity wasn't for me. But despite my declaration, and to my surprise, I was still welcomed and somehow left feeling more peaceful than when I arrived. I went to church a few more times with the same intentions but each time left feeling better than when I arrived.

"When I was eventually able to move again, I'd become a different person."

In February 2017 I agreed to attend an Alpha launch event. A seed was planted that evening. I left with a voice reverberating around my head: "Go and take a proper look. There's nothing to lose but potentially everything to gain!" (These were the words of Mark Greenwood, the speaker for the night.)

The Alpha course immediately felt like a comfortable, open and "safe" environment in which to listen, learn and ask questions. By week three I knew that the life, death and resurrection of Jesus were true. The people

I'd met through church were right all along! I felt overwhelmingly happy for them but also sad that I was beyond redemption. The evening ended too soon and I offered the host pastor Dan a lift home, secretly wanting the opportunity to talk more.

That night my life changed forever. Dan and I sat talking and I gave a very small glimpse into my past. The words "Jesus forgives you but perhaps you need to forgive yourself" had me pinned back in the chair in which I sat. I couldn't speak. I couldn't move. I couldn't understand how Dan had said something that I'd unknowingly been longing to hear for a very long time. I wanted to laugh and cry at the same time but couldn't even make a sound.

When I was eventually able to move again, I'd become a different person. All my burdens had evaporated; the weight on my shoulders was gone. I didn't understand what had just happened but I was completely blown away. That night Jesus had met with me and I felt his overwhelming love for the very first time.

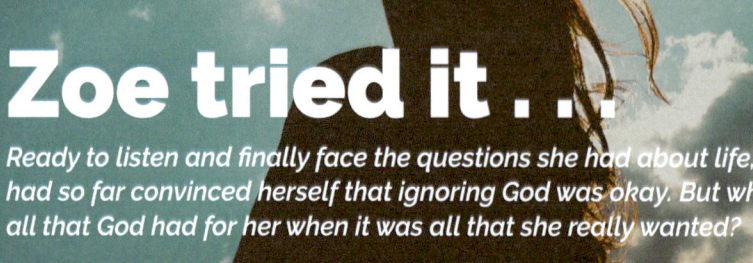

Zoe tried it . . .

Ready to listen and finally face the questions she had about life, Zoe Rayall had so far convinced herself that ignoring God was okay. But why miss out on all that God had for her when it was all that she really wanted?

My parents were heavily involved in the local church. Growing up, church seemed like just another place I had to go, like school, and it certainly didn't seem to have any relevance for me. When I was twenty-three and had just graduated from university, my dad died from cancer. It was a tremendous shock and gave me a valid reason to avoid facing the question of God. I mean, how could God let my dad die? Someone who had been such a big part of the church?

I met my husband in May 2011 and we were engaged and married by May 2013. Six months later we found out we were expecting our first baby. The pregnancy continued without any hiccups. My due date came and went and so I was booked in for an induction. We went to hospital and initial checks stopped my world. A heartbeat couldn't be found. Our beautiful baby girl Grace was stillborn on 4th August 2014.

I took my maternity leave, a year off work to be a parent, only I wasn't able to take care of my baby. I volunteered in a local charity shop and at a drop-in centre. Five months later, I was once again pregnant. A customer at the charity shop asked me if my bump was my first child. I told her all about

Is it Possible?

Grace and the conversation ended up with her inviting me to church. I started going Sunday mornings and would cry at every service. I confided in a few ladies about Grace and my fears for this pregnancy, and they prayed for me and my bump. Jack was born on 23rd September 2015 via caesarean section and, although he had a bit of a wobbly start, he was a healthy baby.

"Wow! A Father?"

Mum's health had been deteriorating, but she did her best to hide it from family and friends. When Jack was seven months old Mum was admitted to hospital; less than a week later she died peacefully. At this time the church I was going to advertised a "Reason to Believe" course with Mark Greenwood. OK, I thought, I'm ready to listen and finally face the questions I had about God. Something Mark said during his course hit home with me, "You can convert at the last minute but then you're missing out on knowing God, a Father who loves us and wants the best for us." Wow! A Father? I had forgotten what it felt like to have one.

But, of course, life took over and again God was put on the back burner. In February 2017 we moved back to the village where I grew up. It was a tough year and put a real strain on our marriage. Surrounded by constant reminders of my parents, being first-time parents to a toddler and visiting the village graveyard where my parents and daughter were buried, resulted in me snapping at my husband one minute and crying the next. I started asking myself the big questions: What is life all about? Why are we here? What is the point? In the end my husband suggested I talk to someone. I agreed but I knew that counselling couldn't answer all my questions. The vicar's wife organised for the church's outreach worker to meet with me, enabling me to work through the emotional rollercoaster I'd been on at the same time as exploring the big questions about God. At a church service in December 2017 there was a pamphlet which talked about life being like a puzzle and it made sense. I prayed the acceptance prayer in the pamphlet.

Since becoming a Christian I have found a sense of peace which I could never quite find before. I feel as though the pieces of my life's jigsaw are fitting together; my life matters and is part of God's plan.

Is it Possible?

Would you consider trying it?

In AD 303 Roman Emperor Diocletian ordered all copies of the books of the Bible to be destroyed. He thought he'd succeeded and even had a medal engraved that said, "The Christian religion is destroyed." But it was Diocletian who died not the Bible or Christianity.

Voltaire was a Frenchman who lived in the 1700s. He was a famous writer, but he didn't believe in the Bible. He predicted that within a hundred years the Bible would be gone. Fifty years after his death, the printing press he had owned was being used to print Bibles and the house he lived in was made into a centre for distributing them.

It is true to say that Christianity has been tried and tested down through the centuries, across the globe, with people of all ages and social standings. In fact I am confident of this: there is someone, somewhere in this world that would be similar to you and has found that it works.

Many have tried to get rid of Christianity and the Bible but have failed in their attempts. It is factual to say the Bible has been, and remains, the best-selling book ever. Is it possible that this is because it contains something that has the power to transform individuals and cultures? Does it contain something that no other book – religious or otherwise – contains? Could it be worth a read?

Is the Bible and Christianity just what you are looking for? Why not find out for yourself? The only way you will test it for yourself, is to try it for yourself.

Is it Possible?

The latest verified statistic shows that by the end of 2019 there were just over 2.5 billion Christians on the planet. Christianity is rising faster than ever before.

(The Center for the Study of Global Christianity at Gordon-Conwell Theological Seminary at the end of 2019)

Is it possible that . . . ?

Sir Arthur Charles Clarke was an English science-fiction writer, science writer, futurist, inventor, undersea explorer and television-series host. He co-wrote the screenplay for the 1968 film *2001: A Space Odyssey*, one of the most influential films of all time.

He said,

"For every man's education should be a process which continues all his life. We have to abandon as swiftly as possible the idea that schooling is something restricted to youth. How can it be, in a world where half the things a man knows at 20 are no longer true at 40 – and half the things he knows at 40 hadn't been discovered when he was 20?"

One of my friends, when he tells me something I don't know or, conversely, I tell him something he doesn't know, loves to say, "Every day's a school day." It always makes me smile and remember that to learn something new is not an insult to my intellect but rather is an addition to my intellect. Would you be willing to allow this moment – this book – to be a school day for you? Rather than see it as a challenge to your intellect, could you see it as an ingredient to your intellect?

Is it Possible?

Imagine the circle here contains the knowledge of the whole world. Place a dot in it – this represents your knowledge.

As you can see, there is a lot that exists and is true but you don't know about it.

Is it Possible?

Is it possible that God does exist but that you don't know it yet?

A new study has found that it's nothing more than good luck that has kept our world full of life. Pure chance is the reason that planet Earth has stayed habitable for billions of years. Scientists at the University of Southampton have carried out a mass simulation of climate evolution of 100,000 randomly generated planets.

Professor Toby Tyrrell, a specialist in Earth system science, said the results of the study, published in the Nature Research journal *Communications Earth & Environment*, suggested chance is a major factor in determining whether planets such as Earth can continue to nurture life over billions of years. He said, "A continuously stable and habitable climate on Earth is quite puzzling. Our neighbours, Mars and Venus, do not have habitable temperatures, even though Mars once did." Earth not only has a habitable temperature today, but has kept this at all times across three to four billion years – an extraordinary span of geological time.

What if it wasn't luck or chance but rather it was someone who wants it that way so that it can thrive? What if rather than "just happens" it's meant to be that way? Is it possible?

What if you could go on a journey to find out if he does exist? And what if that journey was worth it?

Is it Possible?

The Atheist Bus Campaign

Launched in January 2019 and originally in London, posters were placed on buses saying, "There's probably no god. Now stop worrying and enjoy your life." The campaign then spread throughout the UK and the world.

The use of the word "probably" is very honest. You see they didn't say "definitely" as that would have been a step of faith for them. As Richard Dawkins states in *The God Delusion*, saying "there's no God" is taking a "faith" position. He writes, "Atheists do not have faith; and reason alone could not propel one to total conviction that anything definitely does not exist." I love their honesty, but being honest led Atheists to say it's possible that God does exist but you just don't know him.

The use of the phrase "Now stop worrying and enjoy your life" is very interesting. You see, at the heart of the Christian message is the understanding that we not only believe in God, we also believe that in doing that we find true and lasting fulfilment and peace i.e. the ability to enjoy ourselves and not worry.

I have lost count of the number of people who have become Jesus followers and said the words, "If I'd have known it was like this, I'd have done it sooner."

What if God possibly does exist and that by connecting with him you become all you want to be and that he intended you to be? Even the Humanists and Atheists have to admit it's possible!

Stop the bus and ask if it is possible that God exists.

JESUS
did die and come back to life

What if you could go on a journey to find out if he did? And what if that journey was worth it?

Did you know that no serious historian would deny the existence of Jesus? Writers such as Tacitus, Josephus, Pliny, Suetonius and others all agree to the main facts about the existence of Jesus, even mentioning about his death and resurrection and the amazing things he did.

The Roman historian Tacitus wrote around AD 115 concerning the great fire of Rome and Nero's attempt to fasten the blame on to the Christians: "Christus from whom they take their name had been executed by sentence of the procurator Pontius Pilate when Tiberius was governor."

The great Jewish historian Josephus wrote about the history of the Jewish nation around AD 90. He tells us: "At this time there was a wise man who was called Jesus. And his conduct was good and he was known to be virtuous. And many people from among the Jews and from other nations became his disciples. Pilate condemned him to be crucified and to die. And those who had become his disciples did not abandon his discipleship. They reported that he had appeared to them and that three days after his crucifixion he was alive."

Historians tell us Jesus lived and died and that his disciples claimed that he came back to life. We readily accept what history says about Julius Caesar (for whom there is less evidence) but we don't accept what it says of Jesus Christ of whom there is significantly more evidence. Shouldn't all historical evidence be treated in the same way, even that which refers to Jesus?

EVIDENCE

According to the Guinness World Records the most successful lawyer, Sir Lionel Luckhoo, senior partner of Luckhoo & Luckhoo of Georgetown, Guyana, succeeded in getting 245 successive murder-charge acquittals between 1940 and 1985. He said,

"I say unequivocally that the resurrection of Jesus Christ is so overwhelming that it compels acceptance by proof which leaves absolutely no room for doubt."

Frank Morison was an American lawyer with an incredible mind for detail. He set out to write a book to disprove the resurrection, to show once and for all that what Christians claimed happened to Jesus after he was crucified, just wasn't true.

Well he did write a book, and he called it *Who Moved the Stone?* In it he talks about what he set out to disprove and how he ended up discovering that it actually happened. The first chapter of the book is called "The Book that Refused to be Written" and in it he tells his story. The rest of the book is dedicated to the evidence that turned him.

Is it Possible?

In 1998 Lee Strobel, a reporter for the *Chicago Tribune* and a graduate of Yale Law School, published a book called *The Case for Christ: A Journalist's Personal Investigation of the Evidence for Jesus.* His wife had become a Christian whilst he himself was an Atheist.

He set out to show that the key claims of Christianity – that Jesus was the Son of God, the accuracy of the New Testament and the historicity of Jesus' resurrection – were false. However, he was unable to refute these claims to his satisfaction. He also became a Christian.

Of course this is no new thing. Down through the ages there have been those who have tried to discredit the person of Jesus and yet in their quest they have been stopped short. What's remarkable about Morison – and those like him – is that he had a bias against it being true and tried to support his bias. The evidence he found smashed through his bias – I think that's even more compelling.

Some of the greatest minds that ever lived, as well as those that are alive today, believe that not only did Jesus live and die but that he came back to life. These are people whose minds are trained to research and analyse evidence in great detail, much more than you and I.

EVIDENCE

Is it Possible?

It is all true, and totally relevant to you?

What if you could go on a journey to find out if it is? And what if that journey was worth it?

During a battle in the American Civil War, General John Sedgewick squinted at the enemy gun and announced, "They couldn't hit an elephant at that distance." These were his very last words before the same guns blasted him to death.

Ever heard the saying "Never say never"? It's good to be open minded, especially when it's to your benefit and a matter of life and death.

Do you believe in flying cows?

A fisherman on the Aral Sea was enjoying the calm weather and the warm sun when his peace was disturbed by a flying cow. Out of the blue this Friesian landed on his boat, destroying it and almost drowning him. Of course no one believed him and his adventure was thought to be a practical joke. The insurance company refused to pay him for his boat and it was even reported in the newspapers that he told the tallest of stories. Until, that is, the US Airforce admitted that a cow in one of their huge transport planes had gone mad and had been jettisoned over the Aral Sea.

Sometimes you have to believe the unbelievable, however unbelievable it may seem.

Is it Possible?

A chef in a hotel in Switzerland lost a finger in a meat-cutting machine and, after a little hopping around, he submitted a claim to his insurance company. The company, suspecting negligence, sent one of its men to have a look for himself. He tried the machine and lost a finger. The chef's claim was approved. Sometimes the only way to prove it is to experience it.

I get that from a distance the claims of Christianity can look a bit unbelievable. I get that it's tricky to get your head round some stuff – I'm still trying! But what I also know is this: there are lots of things in the world that I don't understand but that never stops me benefiting from them. I know nothing about electricity other than when I connect to it, it gives me power and joy in life – and that will do for me.

> **Dr Ian Macreadie is a highly respected scientist. He is at the forefront of research in a field which to many minds is linked to evolution. He is a highly regarded Australian researcher into molecular biology and microbiology, author of 60 research papers, principal research scientist at the Biomolecular Research Institute of Australia's Commonwealth Scientific and Industrial Research Organisation (CSIRO), national secretary of the Australian Society for Biochemistry and Molecular Biology, and he is a Christian.**
>
> **Most university professors have one earned doctorate, some members of the creation movement (e.g. A.E. Wilder-Smith) have the rare distinction of three doctorates.**
>
> **World-renowned scientist Francis Collins is an American physician-geneticist who discovered the genes associated with a number of diseases. He is the director of the Human Genome project and he is a Bible-believing Christian.**

I do find it helpful when people who know more than I do also have no trouble believing. You don't have to wait till you can get your head around God before you follow him. In fact if I understood everything about God I wouldn't want to follow him, he wouldn't be that impressive!

Take it from me and some incredible brains out there, you don't need to throw your brain away to believe it is all true and totally relevant. You aren't committing some sort of intellectual suicide by becoming a Christian.

Big yes, little yes, healthy maybe

Is it Possible?

George Lucas is best known for creating *Star Wars* and the Indiana Jones movies. He said in an interview, "If you haven't enough interest in the mysteries of life, to ask the question, is there a God or is there not a God?, that for me is the worst thing." He was then asked if he had an opinion, or if he was looking, to which he replied, "Well, I think there is a God." He also said that young people need to have an opinion on this.

C.S. Lewis held academic positions at Oxford and Cambridge universities. He was an Atheist who converted to theism two years before he converted to Christianity. He's probably best known for writing *The Chronicles of Narnia*. He said, "Christianity, if false, is of no importance, and if true, of infinite importance, the only thing it cannot be is moderately important."

Having travelled for over three decades speaking about life with God I have had the joy of seeing tens of thousands start the journey of not only discovering God but actually discovering life. I have lost count of how many people I have met who have been transformed for the better because of this belief in God. A sadness for me is that they have often said, "If I knew it was like this, I would have tried it sooner." Sad because it's all true and therefore of infinite importance.

I started on the front cover of this book asking the question, "Is it possible?" and also on the back saying, "Maybe". If there is any chance it's true you owe it to yourself to find out. Afford yourself the luxury – it's just way too good to miss out.

It is a journey and not a leap. It only takes one small step to begin to consider thinking it all through. May I invite you today to take a step and at the very least invite you to become a "Healthy Maybe".

Is it Possible?

Let me introduce you to Big Yes, Little Yes, Healthy Maybe.

Big Yes

Many people have said a "Big Yes" to God and decided to follow him and his ways. They have asked God to forgive them for leaving him out of their life and for doing their own thing. They have embraced Jesus' death on the cross and his coming back to life, thus receiving his forgiveness and new life and, in so doing, understand that God wants them to make a difference in the world as they connect with him.

Would you be interested in finding out how you can connect with God?

Little Yes

Many people have made an intentional decision to find out more, to investigate whether Christianity is true. Sometimes it's because they are thinking about God and sometimes it's simply because they are thinking about life.

Would you be interested in finding out how you can investigate Christianity?

Healthy Maybe

Many people consider themselves open minded but don't always apply that stance to Christianity. A Healthy Maybe is someone who is willing to become open minded about Christianity, or if they are already open minded, they make a commitment to stay so and maybe willing to chat about it openly.

Would you be interested in becoming or staying open minded?

If you are a

Big Yes, Little Yes or Healthy Maybe

Speak to the person who gave you this book

or connect with me at:

revmarkgreenwood@gmail.com

We would love to help you on your journey.

Is it Possible?

See the full picture